Tozer's Little Instruction Book

HONOR
B O O K S

P.O. Box 55388
Tulsa, OK 741

D0709027

Tozer's Little Instruction Book
ISBN 1-56292-161-4
Copyright © 1996 by Honor Books, Inc.
P.O. Box 55388
Tulsa, OK 74155

Aidan Wilson (A.W.) Tozer was a man of humble beginnings who served God as a preacher and prophet to the American evangelical church in this century. His preaching of profound thought and precise words challenged even the most marginal Christian to pursue the "deeper life" of communion with God. Though he only had a grammar school education, he was extremely well read and self taught in his quest for intimacy with God. He edited a magazine and authored numerous books.

As pastor of Southside Alliance church in Chicago, Tozer was known for denouncing weak and lifeless Christianity that imitated much of the world's ways. To illustrate what the complete surrender to and union with God involved, he often borrowed the writings of classic Christian writers including church fathers and even those of medieval mystics. His lessons were a unique blend of scathing criticisms of a complacent church and a call to embrace the deep love and forgiveness of a majestic God.

STARS IN THE UNIVERSE

God shines in many ways throughout His universe…he shines best of all in the lives of men and women He created and then redeemed.

You made him a little lower than the heavenly being and crowned him with glory and honor!

PSALM 8:5

NO TRENDY CHRISTMAS

All of the Christians I meet who are amounting to anything for God are Christians who are very much out of key with their age— very, very much out of tune with their generation.

Do not conform any longer to the pattern of this world, but be transformed by the renewing of your mind.

ROMANS 12:2

THE MIRACLE PILL?

People testify about their search for the deeper Christian life and it sounds as though they would like to be able to get it in pill form.

He has showed you, O man, what is good. And what does the Lord require of you? To act justly and to love mercy and to walk humbly with your God.

MICAH 6:8

STRAIGHT FROM THE HEART

The things that are closest to our hearts are the things we talk about, and if God is close to your heart, you will talk about Him.

Let love and faithfulness never leave you, bind them around your neck, write them on the tablet of your heart.

PROVERBS 3:3

DID YOU KNOW?

At seventeen, Tozer heard a street evangelist
preach the Gospel. He went to his attic and
received Christ as his personal Savior.

NO CARNAL KNOWLEDGE

The Bible is the easiest book in the world to understand—one of the easiest for the spiritual mind but one of the hardest for the carnal mind.

The man without the Spirit does not accept the things that come from the Spirit of God, for they are foolishness to him…because they are spiritually discerned.

1 CORINTHIANS 2:14

THE HORSE WHO GAVE UP

The Lord isn't angry with your body, because your body is just a poor horse you ride until it crumbles under you and you go off to heaven.

The life I live in the body, I live by faith in the Son of God, who loved me and gave Himself for me.

GALATIANS 2:20

GODLIKE BEINGS

The most godlike thing in the universe is the soul of man.

Then God said, "Let us make man in our image, in our likeness."

GENESIS 1:26

THE KEY TO THE DOOR

The final key to our lives should be turned over to Jesus Christ.

Let us fix our eyes on Jesus, the author and perfecter of our faith.
HEBREWS 12:2

WONDER-WORKING POWER

It is hard for us to accept the majestic simplicity of this constant, wonder-working Jesus.

Jesus answered, "I did tell you, but you do not believe. The miracles I do in my Father's name speak for me, but you do not believe."

JOHN 10:25-26

DID YOU KNOW?

Two years after they met, Ada Pfautz prayed for
him to be filled with the Holy Spirit. One year
later she became his wife.

LOVE HIM FOR HIMSELF

How can God do His work in people who seem to think that Christianity is just another way of getting things from God?

For we are God's workmanship, created in Christ Jesus to do good works, which God prepared in advance for us to do.

EPHESIANS 2:10

BEING OVER DOING

Being has ceased to have much appeal for people and *doing* engages almost everyone's attention. Modern Christians...know almost nothing about the inner life.

Cease striving and know that I am God.

PSALM 46:10 NASB

NO FAVORITE DISCIPLES

There is nothing that Jesus has ever done for any of His disciples that He will not do for any other of His disciples.

―――――――

Greater love has no one than this, that he lay down his life for his friends.

JOHN 15:13

THE FAITH TO FORGET

Reason cannot say, "My sins are gone," but faith knows that they are forgiven and forgotten.

If we confess our sins, He is faithful and just and will forgive us our sins and purify us from all unrighteousness.

1 JOHN 1:9

PROVEN PROMISES

Faith rests upon character. Faith must rest in confidence upon the One who made the promise.

You know with all your heart and soul that not one of all the good promises the Lord your God gave you has failed.

JOSHUA 23:14

DIVINE URGES

We pursue God because, and only because, He has first put an urge within us that spurs us to the pursuit.

For it is by grace you have been saved, through faith — and this not from yourselves, it is the gift of God.

EPHESIANS 2:8

QUANTITY TIME

God can be known satisfactorily only as we devote time to Him.

I love those who love me, and those who seek me find me.

PROVERBS 8:17

PATIENT WITH DUST

You can put all of your confidence in God. He is not angry with you, His dear child! He is not waiting to pounce on you in judgment — He knows that we are dust and He is loving and patient toward us.

The Lord is not slow...He is patient with you, not wanting anyone to perish, but everyone to come to repentance.

2 PETER 3:9

DID YOU KNOW?

Because Tozer relied on voluntary love offerings
for his salary, he had to trust God for food during
the early years of his marriage.

LOST AND FOUND

In the Kingdom of God the surest way to lose something is to try to protect it, and the best way to keep it is to let it go.

Whoever finds his life will lose it, and whoever loses his life for my sake will find it.

MATTHEW 10:39

ARTIFICIALLY WIRED

This is a blasé generation. People have been overstimulated to the place where their nerves are jaded and their tastes corrupted. Natural things have been rejected to make room for things artificial. The sacred has been secularized, the holy vulgarized and worship converted into a form of entertainment.

Their land is full of idols; they bow down to the work of their hands, to what their fingers have made.

ISAIAH 2:8

SMILES BEHIND CLOUDS

The smiling face of God is always turned toward us — but the cloud of concealment is of our own making.

Let the light of your face shine upon us, O Lord.

PSALM 4:6

GOD IS OUR BENEFIT

There is a place in the religious experience where we love God for Himself alone, with never a thought of His benefits.

Your ways, O God, are holy. What god is so great as our God?

PSALM 77:13

A LOVING ECCENTRIC

The only eccentricity [peculiar trait] that I can discover in the heart of God is that a God such as He is should love sinners such as we are.

But God demonstrates his own love for us in this: While we were still sinners, Christ died for us.

ROMANS 5:8

A GREAT CHARACTER

True greatness lies in character, not in ability or position.

———

Blessed are they who keep his statutes and seek him with all their heart.

PSALM 119:2

HAPPILY HOLY

The true Christian ideal is not to be happy but to be holy.

It is written, "Be holy, because I am holy."
1 PETER 1:16

DID YOU KNOW?

Though not a recluse, he was shy and retiring with few close friends. As a "mystic," he spent much time alone with God.

IT'S ALL DELUXE

The Spirit-filled life is not a special, deluxe edition of Christianity. It is part and parcel of the total plan of God for His people.

He anointed us, set his seal of ownership on us, and put his Spirit in our hearts.

2 CORINTHIANS 1:21-22

SHINING APPLES

The believer knows that in himself he is nothing, but even while he is humbly telling the Lord that he is nothing, he knows very well that he is the apple of God's eye.

———————

Keep me as the apple of your eye.
PSALM 17:8

CONTROLLED EXCITEMENT?

There also seems to be a chilling fear of holy enthusiasm among the people of God. We try to tell how happy we are — but we remain so well controlled that there are very few waves of glory experienced in our midst.

Do not put out the Spirit's fire.

1 THESSALONIANS 5:19

CREATED BUT NOT SUSTAINED

I have no doubt that historians will conclude that we of the twentieth century had intelligence enough to create a great civilization but not the moral wisdom to preserve it.

_____

For it is written: "I will destroy the wisdom of the wise; the intelligence of the intelligent I will frustrate."

1 CORINTHIANS 1:19

FROM LIQUID TO SOLID

God salvages the individual by liquidating him and then raising him again to newness of life.

God, who is rich in mercy, made us alive with Christ... and...raised us up with Christ.

EPHESIANS 2:4-6

HELP OTHERS HELP THEMSELVES

In a very real sense no man can teach another; he can only aid him to teach himself.

———

Instruct a wise man and he will be wiser still; teach a righteous man and he will add to his learning.

PROVERBS 9:9

WE ARE WHAT WE LOVE

Not only are we all in process of becoming; we are becoming what we love.

We will in all things grow up into him who is the Head, that is, Christ.

EPHESIANS 4:15

BLOWING A FORTUNE

The man who dies out of Christ...has squandered a rare fortune and at the last he stands for a fleeting moment and looks around, a moral fool...who has lost...his soul, his life, his peace, his total, mysterious personality, his dear and everlasting all.

What good is it for a man to gain the whole world, yet forfeit his soul?

MARK 8:36

All that is worthwhile in Christianity
is a miracle.

ONE BIG MIRACLE

*This is how the birth of Jesus Christ
came about: His mother Mary
was pledged to be married to Joseph,
but before they came together,
she was found to be with child
through the Holy Spirit.*

MATTHEW 1:18

*The
Christian
Classics
Series*

DID YOU KNOW?

He spent three years preaching
through the gospel of John.

NEW BEGINNINGS

God saw not only what we were —
He was faithful in seeing what we
could become. He took away the
curse of being and gave us the
glorious blessing of becoming.

*Inwardly we are being
renewed day by day.*

2 CORINTHIANS 4:16

MIND OVER WHAT MATTERS

In that great and terrible day, there will be those white with shock when they find that they have depended upon a mental assent to Christianity instead of upon the miracle of the new birth.

For God so loved the world that he gave his one and only Son, that whoever believes in him shall not perish but have eternal life.

JOHN 3:16

EXPERIENCE ...THEN PREACH

There isn't anything quite so chilling, quite so disheartening as a man without the Holy Spirit preaching about the Holy Spirit.

And if anyone does not have the Spirit of Christ, he does not belong to Christ.

ROMANS 8:9

EMPTY SUCCESS

A good personality and a shrewd knowledge of human nature are all that any man needs to be a success in religious circles today.

Not many of you should presume to be teachers, my brothers, because you know that we who teach will be judged more strictly.

JAMES 3:1

REVIVAL OF MORALS

I contend that whatever does not raise the moral standard of the church or community has not been a revival from God.

Revive us, and we will call on your name.

PSALM 80:18

TRUST AND OBEY

Salvation apart from obedience is unknown in the sacred Scriptures.

Those who obey his commands live in him, and he in them.

1 JOHN 3:24

SHRUNKEN HEARTS

One of the world's worst tragedies is that we allow our hearts to shrink until there is room in them for little beside ourselves.

———

Today, if you hear his voice, do not harden your hearts.

PSALM 95:7-8

WHAT REALLY COUNTS

God waits for your faith and your love, and He doesn't ask whose interpretation of Scripture you have accepted.

———————

Love the Lord your God with all your heart and with all your soul and with all your mind.

MATTHEW 22:37

DID YOU KNOW?

Three of Tozer's six sons served in the Armed Forces,
and two of them were wounded in action.

WHO LOVES THE WORLD?

You can be a hypocrite and love the world.
You can be a deceived ruler in the
religious system and love the world.
You can be a cheap, snobbish,
modern Christian and love the world.
But you cannot be a genuine
Bible Christian and love the world.

*Do not love the world or anything in the world.
If anyone loves the world, the love of
the Father is not in him.*

1 JOHN 2:15

EAT YOUR OWN FOOD

You cannot rest on another person's testimony. You might just as well try to get fat on what someone else eats as to try to get in heaven on someone else's religious experience.

I tell you...unless you repent, you too will all perish.

LUKE 13:3

HOLY FEELINGS

Worship means "to feel in the heart."

I urge you, brothers, in view of God's mercy, to offer your bodies as living sacrifices, holy and pleasing to God — this is your spiritual act of worship.

ROMANS 12:1

WORSHIP THAT IS ETERNAL

Out of enraptured, admiring, adoring, worshiping souls, then, God does His work. The work done by a worshiper will have eternity in it.

Fear God, and give him glory, because the hour of his judgment has come. Worship him who made the heavens, the earth, the sea and the springs of waters.

REVELATION 14:7

RIGHTEOUS YOUTH

One of our greatest tasks is to demonstrate to the young people of this generation that there is nothing stupid about righteousness.

Then men will say, "Surely the righteous still are rewarded; surely there is a God who judges the earth."

PSALM 58:11

WORTHLESS WORLDLY PRAISE

The meek man cares not at all who is greater than he, for he has long ago decided that the esteem of the world is not worth the effort.

Blessed are the meek, for they will inherit the earth.

MATTHEW 5:5

FOUND BUT STILL SEEKING

To have found God and still to pursue Him is the soul's paradox of love.

———————

He who pursues righteousness and love finds life, prosperity, and honor.

PROVERBS 21:21

It is doubtful we can be Christian in anything unless we are Christian in everything.

ALL OR NOTHING

Finally, brothers, whatever is true, whatever is noble, whatever is right, whatever is pure, whatever is lovely, whatever is admirable — if anything is excellent or praise-worthy — think about such things...And the God of peace will be with you.

PHILIPPIANS 4:8-9

HEALING THANK-FULNESS

Thankfulness that is put into words has a healing effect upon the soul and has a good effect upon those who hear.

———————

We always thank God for all of you, mentioning you in our prayers.

1 THESSALONIANS 1:2

DID YOU KNOW?

He was a friend of the great preacher from England, D. Martin Lloyd-Jones, who wanted Tozer to preach overseas.

LIVE ACTION

One hundred religious persons knit into a unity by careful organization do not constitute a church any more than eleven dead men make a football team.

———————

Religion that God our Father accepts as pure and faultless is this: to look after orphans and widows in their distress and to keep oneself from being polluted by the world.

JAMES 1:27

LIVING FOSSILS?

When the Holy Spirit is ignored or rejected, religious people are forced either to do their own creating or to fossilize completely.

So I say, live by the Spirit, and you will not gratify the desires of the sinful nature.

GALATIANS 5:16

POSITIVELY RIGHT

Too many of our religious convictions are negative. We act not from a positive conviction that something is right, but from a feeling that the opposite is wrong.

For we maintain that a man is justified by faith apart from the works of the Law.

ROMANS 3:28 NASB

THE CAT KNOWS TOO

As the evangelists tell us, even the cat will know it when the head of the house is converted.

They replied, "Believe in the Lord Jesus, and you will be saved — you and your household."

ACTS 16:31

WORD AND DEED

Most religious people have been guilty of multiplying words as substitutes for worthy deeds, and of all such the writer of these lines is probably the worst offender.

A man of knowledge uses words with restraint.

PROVERBS 17:27

*CHRIST
RULES
FOREVER*

Christ will be standing upright, tall and immortal, after the tumult and the shouting dies and the captains and the kings lie stretched side by side, the "cause" that made them famous forgotten and their whole significance reduced to a paragraph in a history book.

Hallelujah! For our Lord God Almighty reigns. Let us rejoice and be glad and give him glory!

REVELATION 19:6-7

REASON MUST KNEEL

Love and faith are at home in the mystery of the Godhead. Let reason kneel in reverence outside.

You hem me in—behind and before; you have laid your hand upon me. Such knowledge is too wonderful for me, too lofty for me to attain.

PSALM 139:5-6

ANXIOUS AND HURRIED

God has not bowed to our nervous haste nor embraced the methods of our machine age. The man who would know God must give time to Him.

Be still before the Lord and wait patiently for him.

PSALM 37:7

THEOLOGY IS NOT ENOUGH

The devil is a better theologian than any of us and is a devil still.

You believe that there is one God. Good! Even the demons believe that—and shudder.

JAMES 2:19

EMPTY ENTERTAINMENT

Much that passes for New Testament Christianity is little more than objective truth sweetened with song and made palatable by religious entertainment.

See to it that no one takes you captive through hollow and deceptive philosophy.

COLOSSIANS 2:8

THE BASIC "NEVER NEVERS"

Now there are five vows I have in mind which we do well to make and keep. 1. Deal thoroughly with sin. 2. Never own anything—get rid of the sense of possessing. 3. Never defend yourself. 4. Never pass anything on about anybody else that will hurt him. 5. Never accept any glory.

Put to death, therefore, whatever belongs to your earthly nature: sexual immorality, impurity, lust, evil desires and greed, which is idolatry.
Colossians 3:5

VICTORY FIRST

The Lord cannot fully bless a man until He has first conquered him.

—————

He will bless those who fear the Lord.
PSALM 115:13

DID YOU KNOW?

In sermon preparation he might spend hours
trying to find one precise word or phrase.

NOISE NEVER ENDS

The need for solitude and quietness was never greater than it is today.

But I have stilled and quieted my soul; like a weaned child with its mother, like a weaned child is my soul within me.

PSALM 131:2

THIS CROSS IS FOR YOU

Carry your own cross but never lay one on the back of another.

If anyone would come after me, he must deny himself and take up his cross and follow me.

MARK 8:34

DON'T GIVE UP THE FIGHT

Compromise will take the pressure off. Satan will not bother a man who has quit fighting. But the cost of quitting will be a life of peaceful stagnation. We sons of eternity just cannot afford such a thing.

Therefore, my dear friends… continue to work out your salvation with fear and trembling.

PHILIPPIANS 2:12

LIVE WHAT YOU PRAY

Our prayers are only as powerful as our lives. In the long pull we pray only as well as we live.

The prayer of a righteous man is powerful and effective.

JAMES 5:16

DISCOURAGED DECISIONS

It is a splendid rule to refrain from making decisions when we are discouraged.

———

Wait for the Lord; be strong and take heart and wait for the Lord.

PSALM 27:14

Grace will save a man but it will not save him and his idol.

IDOL BASHING

If you put your detestable idols out of my sight and no longer go astray...then the nations will be blessed by him and in him they will glory.

JEREMIAH 4:1-2

We can afford to suffer now;
we'll have a long eternity to
enjoy ourselves.

SUFFERING IS SHORT

---

*I consider that our present
sufferings are not worth
comparing with the glory that
will be revealed to us.*

ROMANS 8:18

What I believe about God is the most important thing about me.

MY FAITH IS MY IDENTITY

If you confess with your mouth "Jesus is Lord," and believe in your heart that God raised him from the dead, you will be saved.

ROMANS 10:9

DID YOU KNOW?

A young evangelist named Billy Graham
came to him for counsel.

Humility is as scarce as an albino robin.

A RARE BREED

Clothe yourselves with humility toward one another, because "God opposes the proud, but gives grace to the humble."

1 PETER 5:5

RELUCTANT LEADERSHIP

A true and safe leader is likely to be one who has no desire to lead, but is forced into a position of leadership by the inward pressure of the Holy Spirit and the press of the external situation.

Trust in the Lord with all your heart and lean not on your own understanding; in all your ways acknowledge him, and he will make your paths straight.

PROVERBS 3:5-6

LOVING TO OBEY

Our Lord told His disciples that love and obedience were organically united. The final test of love is obedience.

If anyone loves me, he will obey my teaching….He who does not love me will not obey my teaching.

JOHN 14:23-24

The warfare of the Christian is like foreign missions, romantic to talk about but drably realistic to live through.

TOUGH, NOT GLAMOROUS

For though we walk in the flesh, we do not war according to the flesh, for the weapons of our warfare are not of the flesh, but divinely powerful for the destruction of fortresses.

2 CORINTHIANS 10:3-4 NASB

〜 A Wife Remembers 〜

"On the Sunday I joined the church he was an usher and it was he who took me to the front to join. I was a green country girl and was very embarrassed to go with him. I said to a girl I was sitting with, 'That was worse than a wedding,' which he overheard. Oh, he was a handsome, clean-cut young man of eighteen and I was not yet fifteen."

—Ada Pfautz Tozer

RESIDENTS OF THE SANCTUARY

Ransomed man need no longer pause in fear to enter the Holy of Holies. God wills that we should push on into His presence and live our whole life there.

Let us then approach the throne of grace with confidence, so that we may receive mercy and find grace to help us in our time of need.

HEBREWS 4:16

PONDER WHAT YOU READ

You should think ten times more than you read.

But his delight is in the law of the Lord, and on his law he meditates day and night.

PSALM 1:2

ONLY THREE CHANCES

In baseball a player always goes back and sits down after he strikes out. It would help matters in many a church if that rule could be applied to board members.

_____

If anyone does not know how to manage his own family, how can he take care of God's church.

1 TIMOTHY 3:5

STREAMS IN THE DESERT

"Dr. Tozer is to me a classic example of the promise,
'Out of his inmost being shall flow rivers of living water.'"

Leonard Ravenhill

INTOXICATED WITH GOD

There is a tremendous need for prophets in each generation. These are the spiritual originals, the God-intoxicated few, who, in every age, have spoken God's clear message into the duller ears of the multitudes.

Let the one who has my word speak it faithfully.

JEREMIAH 23:28

HIGH TECH HEARTS

The greatest danger we face from this machine age is that we will become engrossed with mechanical gadgets and forget we have hearts. Man cannot live by bread alone nor by machinery alone.

I am the living bread that came down from heaven. If anyone eats of this bread, he will live forever.

JOHN 6:51

FINAL MERCY

Every ransomed man owes his salvation to the fact that during the days of his sinning, God kept the door of mercy open by refusing to accept any of his evil acts as final.

But because of his great love for us, God, who is rich in mercy, made us alive with Christ even when we were dead in transgressions— it is by grace you have been saved.

EPHESIANS 2:4-5

DID YOU KNOW?

After six sons, Tozer was a doting father to his last child
—a daughter named Rebecca born in his later life.

GAZING AWAY

Faith is not a once-done act, but a continuous gaze of the heart at the Triune God.

Therefore, since we are surrounded by such a great cloud of witnesses...let us run with perseverance the race marked out for us.

HEBREWS 12:1

BELIEF IN GOD ALONE

Faith never means gullibility. The man who believes everything is as far from God as the man who refuses to believe anything.

Dear friends, do not believe every spirit, but test the spirits to see whether they are from God, because many false prophets have gone out into the world.

1 JOHN 4:1

REAL FAITH NEVER FAILS

Pseudo faith always arranges a way out to serve in case God fails it.

Continue in your faith, established and firm, not [moving] from the hope held out in the gospel.

COLOSSIANS 1:23

A HOPE AFTER THIS LIFE

God's eternity and man's mortality join to persuade us that faith in Jesus Christ is not optional. For every man it must be Christ, or eternal tragedy.

For the wages of sin is death, but the gift of God is eternal life in Christ Jesus our Lord.

ROMANS 6:23

KEYS TO GOOD SOLDIERING

Deliver me from overeating and late sleeping. Teach me self-discipline that I may be a good soldier of Jesus Christ.

A little sleep, a little slumber, a little folding of the hands to rest—and poverty will come on you like a bandit and scarcity like an armed man.

PROVERBS 6:10-11

MORAL OF THE STORY

The work of a good book is to incite the reader to moral action, to turn his eyes toward God and urge him forward.

Blessed is the one who reads.

REVELATION 1:3

THE PRAYER OF A PREACHER

Pray for me in the light of the pressures of our times.
Pray that I will not just come to a wearied end—
an exhausted, tired old preacher, interested only in
hunting a place to roost. Pray that I will be willing to
let my Christian experience and Christian standards
cost me something right down to the last gasp.

Not that I have already obtained all this, or have already been made perfect, but I press on to take hold of that for which Christ Jesus took hold of me.

PHILIPPIANS 3:12

A RIGHT SPIRIT FIRST

Always it is more important that we retain a right spirit toward others than that we bring them to our way of thinking, even if our way is right.

———————

Accept him whose faith is weak, without passing judgment on disputable matters.

ROMANS 14:1

CHOOSE WISELY

The choices of life, not the compulsions, reveal character.

———————

Choose for yourselves this day whom you will serve.

JOSHUA 24:15

POPULAR BUT WEAK

The Christ of popular Christianity has a weak smile and a halo. He has become Someone-up-There who likes people, at least to some people, and these are grateful but not too impressed. If they need Him, He also needs them.

Look, the Lamb of God, who takes away the sin of the world!

JOHN 1:29

THE HIGHEST HONOR

To be called to follow Christ is a high honor; higher indeed than any honor men can bestow upon each other.

———

With this in mind, we constantly pray for you, that our God may count you worthy of his calling, and that by his power he may fulfill every good purpose of yours.

2 THESSALONIANS 1:11

One of the most stinging criticisms made against Christians is that their minds are narrow and their hearts small.

NARROW MINDS

Do your best to present yourself to God as one approved, a workman who does not need to be ashamed and who correctly handles the word of truth.

2 TIMOTHY 2:15

DID YOU KNOW?

Among his best known books were *The Pursuit of God* (1948) and *The Knowledge of the Holy* (1961).

NEWS OF THE SPIRIT

It might be well for us Christians to listen less to the news commentaries and more to the voice of the Spirit.

Since we live by the Spirit, let us keep in step with the Spirit.

GALATIANS 5:25

SIMPLIFY FOR ETERNITY

We Christians must simplify our lives or lose untold treasures on earth and in eternity.

But seek first his kingdom and his righteousness, and all these things will be given to you.

MATTHEW 6:33

FULLY ALIVE

The Christian believes that in Christ he has died, yet he is more alive than before and he fully expects to live forever.

I have been crucified with Christ and I no longer live, but Christ lives in me.

GALATIANS 2:20

A RELIGIOUS MASCOT?

The popular image of the man of God as a smiling, congenial, asexual religious mascot whose handshake is always soft and whose head is always bobbing in the perpetual Yes of universal acquiescence is not the image found in the Scriptures of truth.

Be strong and courageous. Do not be terrified; do not be discouraged, for the Lord your God will be with you wherever you go.

JOSHUA 1:9

STIR YOUR SOUL

One of the greatest foes of the Christian is religious complacency.

Woe to you who are complacent in Zion.

AMOS 6:1

A GENTLE MASTER

The man who surrenders to Christ exchanges a cruel slave driver for a kind and gentle Master whose yoke is easy and whose burden is light.

For my yoke is easy and my burden is light.
MATTHEW 11:30

IN HIS PLACE

The whole course of the life is upset by failure to put God where He belongs.

All things were created by him and for him. He is before all things, and in him all things hold together.

COLOSSIANS 1:16-17

The cross is rough, and it is deadly, but it is effective.

DEADLY EFFECTIVE

Having canceled out the certificate of debt consisting of decrees against us and which was hostile to us; and He has taken it out of the way, having nailed it to the cross.

COLOSSIANS 2:14 NASB

SEX AND THE SPIRITUAL

For millions the erotic has completely displaced the spiritual.

It is God's will that you should be sanctified: that you should avoid sexual immorality.

1 THESSALONIANS 4:3

GIVE UP AND FORGIVE

To be forgiven, a sin must be forsaken.

He who conceals his transgressions will not prosper, but he who confesses and forsakes them will find compassion.

PROVERBS 28:13 NASB

FREEDOM FIRST

Any nation which for an extended period puts pleasure before liberty is likely to lose the liberty it misused.

Gather together, gather together...before the day of the Lord's wrath comes upon you.

ZEPHANIAH 2:1-2

To God there are no small offerings if they are made in the name of His Son.

BIG-HEARTED GIVING

I tell you the truth, this poor widow has put more into the treasury than all the others. They all gave out of their wealth; but she, out of her poverty, put in everything—all she had to live on.

MARK 12:43-44

DEADLINE FREE PLANS

God never hurries. There are no deadlines against which He must work.

———————

With the Lord one day is like a thousand years, and a thousand years are like a day.

2 PETER 3:8

HAVING IT ALL

God being who He is, the inheritance we receive from Him is limitless—it is all of the universe.

For the world is mine, and all that is in it.

PSALM 50:12

DID YOU KNOW?

He only completed grammar school,
yet both Wheaton College and Houghton College
awarded him honorary doctorates.

BLIND LOVE

The good Christian is in love with one he has never seen, and although he fears and reveres God, he is not afraid of God at all.

Let us then approach the throne of grace with confidence.

HEBREWS 4:16

A GOOD MOOD FOREVER

God never changes moods or cools off in His affections or loses enthusiasm.

Do you not know? Have you not heard? The Everlasting God, the Lord, the Creator of the ends of the earth does not become weary or tired. His understanding is inscrutable.

ISAIAH 40:28 NASB

VOICE OF A FRIEND

The voice of God is a friendly voice. No one need fear to listen to it unless he has already made up his mind to resist it.

I am the God of your father Abraham. Do not be afraid, for I am with you.

GENESIS 26:24

DELIGHTFUL COMPANY

The people of God ought to be the happiest people in all the wide world. People should be coming to us constantly and asking the source of our joy and delight.

Let your light shine before men, that they may see your good deeds and praise your Father in heaven.

MATTHEW 5:16

THE ENERGIZING SPIRIT

No matter what a man does, no matter how successful he seems to be in any field, if the Holy Spirit is not the chief energizer of his activity, it will all fall apart when he dies.

The one who sows to please his sinful nature, from that nature will reap destruction; the one who sows to please the Spirit, from the Spirit will reap eternal life.

GALATIANS 6:8

NO LITTLE PEOPLE

The Kingdom of God is not divided into areas for big, important people and areas for little, unimportant people. Everyone is just as needful in God's sight as any other.

There should be no division in the body, but that its parts should have equal concern for each other.

1 CORINTHIANS 12:25

EVERYBODY COUNTS

Jesus continually placed His emphasis upon the value and worth of the individual.

I tell you that in the same way there will be more rejoicing in heaven over one sinner who repents than over ninety-nine righteous persons who do not need to repent.

LUKE 15:7

SIN IS NOT ENOUGH

Man is bored, because he is too big to be happy with that which sin is giving him. God has made him too great, his potential is too mighty.

―――――――――

Sin is crouching at your door;
it desires to have you,
but you must master it.

GENESIS 4:7

DID YOU KNOW?

He was editor of *The Alliance Weekly*, the official publication
of the Christian and Missionary Alliance Church.

TIED IN KNOTS

We must never underestimate the ability of human beings to get themselves tangled up.

———————

There is a way that seems right to a man, but in the end it leads to death.

PROVERBS 16:25

SOVEREIGN BUT FLEXIBLE

The essence of true religion is spontaneity, the sovereign movings of the Holy Spirit upon and in the free spirit of redeemed man.

Those who are led by the Spirit of God are sons of God.

ROMANS 8:14

137

THE SMELL OF MONEY

The very smell of the currency we pass around indicates where it has been. It smells of itself—as though it could tell its own story of crime and violence and immorality.

For the love of money is a root of all kinds of evil. Some people, eager for money, have wandered from the faith.

1 TIMOTHY 6:10

The knowledge that we are never alone calms the troubled sea of our lives and speaks peace to our souls.

TOGETHER AT SEA

———

God is a refuge and strength, an ever-present help in trouble. Therefore we will not fear.

PSALM 46:1-2

CHARMING PULPITEERS

I feel sorry for the church that decides to call a man to the pulpit because "his personality simply sparkles."

Since an overseer is entrusted with God's work, he must be blameless... hospitable, one who loves what is good, who is self-controlled, upright, holy, and disciplined.

TITUS 1:7-8

EXPERIENCING THE TRINITY

Progress in the Christian life is exactly equal to the growing knowledge we gain of the Triune God in personal experience.

But grow in the grace and knowledge of our Lord and Savior Jesus Christ.

2 PETER 3:18

PAST AND PRESENT

Scholars can interpret the past; it takes prophets to interpret the present.

The spirits of prophets are subject to the control of prophets.

1 CORINTHIANS 14:32

WISHING WE'RE BETTER?

Regret may be no more than self-love. A man may have such a high regard for himself that any failure to live up to his own image of himself disappoints him deeply.

For by the grace given me I say to every one of you: Do not think of yourself more highly that you ought.

ROMANS 12:3

BORED WITH RELIGION

One mark of the low state of affairs among us is religious boredom.

So, because you are lukewarm—neither hot nor cold—I am about to spit you out of my mouth.

REVELATION 3:16

THE COST OF RIGHTEOUSNESS

It appears that too many Christians want to enjoy the thrill of feeling right but are not willing to endure the inconvenience of being right.

I consider everything a loss compared to the surpassing greatness of knowing Christ Jesus my Lord, for whose sake I have lost all things. I consider them rubbish, that I may gain Christ.

PHILIPPIANS 3:8

145

RULES FOR SELF-DISCOVERY

Tozer noted that the following concepts revealed much about a person's character.

1. What we want most.
2. What we think about most.
3. How we use our money.

4. What we do with our leisure time.
5. The company we enjoy.
6. Whom and what we admire.
7. What we laugh at.

*For where your treasure is,
there your heart will be also.*
LUKE 12:34

UNDISCOVERED SELF-DECEPTION

Of all forms of deception self-deception is the most deadly, and of all deceived persons the self-deceived are the least likely to discover the fraud.

———

Do not deceive yourselves.

1 CORINTHIANS 3:18

⌒ TOZER'S CLOSENESS ⌒
TO GOD

"Tozer knelt by his chair, took off his glasses and laid them on the chair. Resting on his bent ankles, he clasped his hands together, raised his face with his eyes closed and began: 'O God, we are before Thee.' With that there came a rush of God's presence that filled the room. We both worshiped in silent ecstasy and wonder and adoration. I've never forgotten that moment, and I don't want to forget it."

—Raymond McAfee

SEALS WITH TEETH

Some churches train their greeters and ushers to smile, showing as many teeth as possible...and when I am greeted by a man [like that], I know I am shaking the flipper of a trained seal.

And if you greet only your brothers, what are you doing more than others? Do not even pagans do that?

MATTHEW 5:47

OLD MAN SIN

The idea that sin is modern is false. There has not been a new sin invented since the beginning of recorded history.

———

Is there anything of which one can say, "Look! This is something new?" It was here already, long ago.

ECCLESIASTES 1:10

The best way to control our thoughts is to offer the mind to God in complete surrender.

SURRENDER YOUR THOUGHTS

Do not conform any longer to the pattern of this world, but be transformed by the renewing of your mind. Then you will be able to test and approve what God's will is—his good, pleasing and perfect will.

ROMANS 12:2

MARRIED TO THE TRUTH

Truth is a glorious but hard mistress. She never consults, bargains or compromises.

For your love is ever before me, and I walk continually in your truth.

PSALM 26:3

HEAVEN IS MORE COMFORTABLE

It is hard to focus upon a better world to come when a more comfortable one than this can hardly be imagined.

Set your minds on things above, not on earthly things.

COLOSSIANS 3:2

SELF-DEVOTED

Men who refuse to worship the true God now worship themselves with tender devotion.

You shall have no other gods before me.

EXODUS 20:3

DID YOU KNOW?

At times he would lay prostrate before God without a word, but just gazing upon Him in worship.

To be right with God has often meant to be in trouble with men.

GOOD TROUBLE

I have given them your word and the world has hated them, for they are not of the world any more than I am of the world.

JOHN 17:14

THE PURPOSES OF FAITH

Faith in one of its aspects moves mountains; in another it gives patience to see promises afar off and wait quietly for their fulfillment.

———

Now faith is the assurance of things hoped for, the conviction of things not seen.

HEBREWS 11:1 NASB

GOD IS OUR GOAL

Remember that the living God is everything. Not success, not victory—but God. Not winning, not losing—but God.

———

But the Lord is the true God; he is the living God, the eternal King.
JEREMIAH 10:10

Additional copies of this book
and other titles from **Honor Books**
are available at your local bookstore:

D.L. Moody's Little Instruction Book
John Wesley's Little Instruction Book
Larry Burkett's Little Instruction Book
Martin Luther's Little Instruction Book
Tozer's Little Instruction Book
God's Little Instruction Book (series)
God's Little Devotional Book (series)

Tulsa, Oklahoma